ESSENTIAL 101 TIPS

WINE

ESSENTIAL TIPS

WINE

Tom Stevenson

DK PUBLISHING, INC.

www.dk.com

A DK PUBLISHING BOOK
www.dk.com
Editor Lesley Malkin
Art Editor Martin Hendry
Series Editor Gillian Roberts
Series Art Editor Clive Hayball
Picture Researcher Melissa Albany
Production Controller Lauren Britton
US Editor Laaren Brown

First American Edition, 1997
10 9
Published in the United States by DK Publishing, Inc.
95 Madison Avenue, New York, New York 10016

Visit us on the World Wide Web at http://www.dk.com

Copyright © 1997 Dorling Kindersley Limited, London

A catalog record is available from the Library of Congress

ISBN 0-7894-1464-3

Text film output by The Right Type, Great Britain
Reproduced by Colourscan, Singapore
Printed by Wing King Tong, Hong Kong

ESSENTIAL TIPS

PAGES 36-41

HOW WINE IS MADE

PAGES 42-43

SPARKLING WINE

PAGES 44-47

FORTIFIED WINE

PAGES 48-53

ASSESSING WINE

WHAT IS WINE?

1 DEFINING WINE

All wine, whether still, sparkling, fortified, or aromatized, is fermented grape juice. It may be red, white, or pink (rosé), and dry, medium, or sweet in style, with an alcohol content of 5.5 to 14 percent. Grape spirit is added to fortified wine, raising the alcohol level to 15–22 percent. Sparkling wine contains trapped carbon dioxide (CO_2) bubbles, which are released on opening.

WINE GRAPES

2 HISTORY OF WINE

Archeological clues suggest that grapes were cultivated as far back as 4000 BC, and although the exact origins of wine-making are uncertain, civilization has merely refined what is a natural process. Stronger glass and tighter stoppers, and Louis Pasteur's research into fermentation in the 19th century, enabled the production of wine to develop into the huge commercial industry that it is today.

PHYLLOXERA VASTATRIX
The vine louse, still to be found in most vineyard soils, devastated the European wine industry in the late 19th century. Tragic at the time, it resulted in the planting of more disease-resistant vines.

FIFTEENTH-CENTURY FRENCH VINEYARD
Tending vines for the making of wine has long been part of the French way of life.

3 SIMPLE ANATOMY OF THE GRAPE

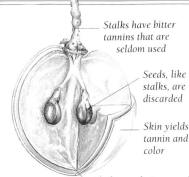

Variations in the taste of wine are for the most part due to the following differences between grape varieties:

- Size: the smaller the grape, the more concentrated its flavor.
- Skin color and thickness: these give wine (especially red and rosé) its color and many of its aromatic qualities.
- Acid/sugar ratio: this determines the wine's sweetness and level of alcohol.

Stalks have bitter tannins that are seldom used

Seeds, like stalks, are discarded

Skin yields tannin and color

Flesh or pulp is pressed to release juice

4 IS CLIMATE IMPORTANT?

Grapes vary slightly in their needs, but vines will usually thrive within certain limits. An average annual temperature of 57–59°F (14–15°C), with a summer average of not less than 66°F (19°C), is ideal. Summer should not be too hot nor autumn too cool. Rain, around 27in (675mm) per year, should fall in winter and spring; too much in summer and autumn can harm the grapes. Bad weather is a worry: frost, strong winds, hail, and heavy rain are major dangers.

SUNSET IN AN AUSTRALIAN VINEYARD
Sunlight, essential to the growing vine, is most valuable for its ripening heat.

WIND MACHINES IN NAPA VALLEY
Frost is a great enemy of the crop. Wind machines help prevent cold from settling.

5 INFLUENCE OF SOIL CONDITIONS

The traditional vineyard adage that the poorer the soil, the better the wine, arises from a vine's need for very well-drained soil. The soil must be able to retain moisture without becoming waterlogged. Warm soils like gravel, sand, and loam retain heat, which speeds ripening, while a cold soil such as clay retards it.

INTERNATIONAL DEBATE
How much effect the nature of the soil has on the resulting wine is the cause of much debate between the Old World, where it is considered vital, and the New World, which minimizes its role.

STONY BURGUNDY SOIL
Stones absorb heat from the sun during the day and radiate it back in the night, which is advantageous in cooler vineyards.

6 TOPOGRAPHY & ASPECT

Topographical variations give rise to microclimates that differ from the overall prevailing climate.
- Slopes, which have concentrated sunlight and better drainage, are more suited to vines than flat land, where the soil may be too fertile.
- Slopes that face south in the northern hemisphere receive more sun, consequently are warmer; the opposite is true in the southern hemisphere. In hot areas, the cool slopes tend to be cultivated.
- Altitude affects temperature, too: grapes take longer to ripen in higher, cooler vineyards.

TERRACED VINEYARD IN ITALY
The increased sunlight and good drainage offered by otherwise inhospitable steep slopes, such as these, are ideal for vines.

7 THE GRAPE'S LIFE CYCLE

Grape varieties bud at different times

When the dormant vines begin to weep sap, spring growth is about to begin. Buds emerge first, followed over the next eight weeks by foliage and flowers. The vines are generally pruned twice a year. All pollinated and fertilized flowers become grapes, which gradually change color as they ripen. Harvesting takes place in fall.

EMBRYO GRAPES
Spraying with fertilizers and pesticides, preferably organic, starts now and continues until the harvest.

RIPENING FRUIT
Foliage around the ripening fruit is sometimes thinned to expose grapes to more warmth, light, and air.

ICE WINE
Occasionally, grapes are harvested in winter when they are frozen. They make a sweet but balanced wine.

8 WHAT IS NOBLE ROT?

If conditions in fall are warm and humid enough, grapes left on the vine may be infected by a fungus called *Botrytis cinerea*, or noble rot. Botrytized grapes are shriveled and dehydrated, but their sweetness is concentrated. The best examples of very sweet dessert wines that are made from botrytized grapes are produced in Bordeaux and Germany.

MOST NOBLE VARIETIES
Noble rot affects Riesling, Sauvignon blanc, Chenin blanc, Sémillon, and Gewürztraminer favorably.

Botrytized grapes make lusciously sweet wines

GRAPE VARIETIES

9 WHICH GRAPES MAKE WINE?

Grapes make up a large, diverse plant family. All the classic wine-making grapes come from the species *Vitis vinifera*, which yields the largest and sweetest fruits. Thousands of varieties of *Vitis vinifera* exist. The grape variety determines the character of any given wine, although growing conditions and the wine-making process will affect the final result.

SPECIES *vinifera*

Chardonnay, Riesling, and Pinot noir are well-known examples of Vitis vinifera *varieties*

Other species are used for wine, but none is as successful as vinifera

GENUS *Vitis*

Vitis *is the only genus of all the grape family genera that is important for wine-making*

BOTANICAL FAMILY *Vitaceae*

Thick-skinned fruits are small and blue in color

10 CABERNET SAUVIGNON

This is the most well-known black grape variety in the world. Along with Merlot, with which it is often blended, it is the most important Bordeaux variety and is successful in the New World, too. The grapes are high in tannins, so Cabernet sauvignon wines age well (especially if oaked), but need time to mature. At best, the wines are rich in color, aroma, and depth, and in time have a long-lasting flavor, often of blackcurrants.

SAME AGAIN
Grown in many wine regions around the world, this variety always makes wines with a recognizable style and flavor.

11 CHARDONNAY

Unquestionably the most popular white grape variety, this is in part due to its unfussy temperament and versatility for making wine. It is the variety behind classic white Burgundy and one of the three varieties used to make Champagne. Wines from this grape are dry, and light (crisp apple-like flavors) to medium and full bodied (buttery), depending on how they are made.

Chardonnay is easy to cultivate, disease-resistant, and prolific in most conditions

BARREL AGING
Chardonnay responds very well to being aged in oak. This gives the wine a depth of flavor not achieved by other processes.

12 CHENIN BLANC

Very high acidity characterizes these grapes, which need plenty of sun to ripen properly; otherwise the wines are tart. The main regions for Chenin blanc are the Loire, New Zealand, and South Africa. White wines from very dry to sweet (some of them botrytized), as well as sparkling, are produced. Successful dry wines are fresh and fruity, sweet wines well-balanced and honeyed.

Grapes have thin skins and high sugar content

IMPROVING WITH AGE
Aging improves good quality sweet Chenin blanc by bringing out the fruit.

13 Gamay

Beaujolais, which is made from the Gamay grape, is of enormous commercial importance in Burgundy, where it accounts for more than half of all wine produced. Most are uncomplicated, light, fruity reds intended for quaffing when young and fresh. The wine has a distinctive intense pear aroma, which is the result of the production methods, and a raspberry flavor. More serious Beaujolais can be aged.

14 Gewürztraminer

The highly aromatic wines made from this spicy variety are full-bodied whites that can be dry or sweet. They have low acidity and a high alcohol content, often over 13 percent. Alsace produces the finest examples. With its exotic perfume and intense litchi flavor, Gewürztraminer is one of the few wines that will go with spicy food.

Frost is a danger to young buds in spring

Grapes are distinctive pale pink color

15 GRENACHE

On its own, this black grape makes warm, fruity flavored wines with a high alcohol content and aromas of freshly ground black pepper. The grapes are low in tannins, however, so they are often blended with highly tannic grapes such as Cabernet sauvignon or Syrah, which benefits both of these varieties. Southern France, Australia, California, and Spain are the main growing areas.

Grape yields must be carefully controlled to ensure quality

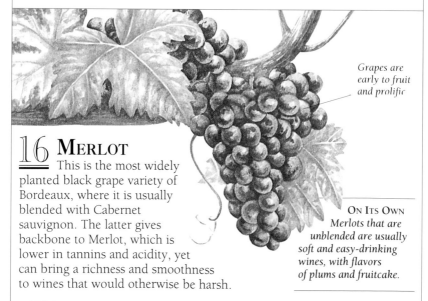

Grapes are early to fruit and prolific

16 MERLOT

This is the most widely planted black grape variety of Bordeaux, where it is usually blended with Cabernet sauvignon. The latter gives backbone to Merlot, which is lower in tannins and acidity, yet can bring a richness and smoothness to wines that would otherwise be harsh.

ON ITS OWN
Merlots that are unblended are usually soft and easy-drinking wines, with flavors of plums and fruitcake.

Conditions must be ideal for the vines to thrive

Low levels of tannin and color in skins

17 PINOT NOIR

This is the grape used to make red Burgundy. It is extremely sensitive to climatic conditions, and yields are not very high, making it both difficult and expensive to produce. Rarely blended, Pinot noir grapes make fairly pale-colored, light- to medium-bodied reds, with a strawberry or raspberry aroma. Best quality Pinot noirs are those from Burgundy; they can be the most sumptuous reds in the world. Some other regions, including New Zealand and Oregon, are starting to enjoy success.

KEY ROLE
Pinot noir is one of the main grape varieties used in Champagne.

18 RIESLING

This classic German grape variety makes some fine white wines all over the world, from bone dry to very sweet. They are light in body and low in alcohol, yet strongly flavored and very long-lived. High acidity always balances any richness, whatever the style of wine. Superb, very sweet white wines are made from Riesling grapes that have been subject to noble rot (*Tip 8*).

Slow ripening is best

Wood is very hard, making the vine frost-resistant

TRUE RIESLING
Riesling's reputation has suffered unfairly in recent years due to similar but inferior grapes being wrongly labeled as Riesling.

PARTNERS IN WINE
The acidity makes this a good blending variety, to add zest to bland wines. If blended, it is most often with Sémillon.

19 SAUVIGNON BLANC

Wines made from this grape are mostly very dry, fresh whites, designed to be drunk young. Their intense taste and aroma, suggestive of green grass and gooseberries (*Tip 70*), make them easy to recognize. Sancerre and Pouilly Fumé, from the Loire, are perhaps the most well-known Sauvignon blancs, but New Zealand also produces some fine examples. The grape variety may appear on the label.

Growth of this vine is very vigorous

20 SÉMILLON

This versatile grape makes a range of white wines, dry to very sweet, particularly notable in Australia and Bordeaux. It is often blended, usually with Sauvignon blanc and also Chardonnay. Dry and blended wines are best when young, but many of the sweeter wines improve with age. Sémillon is perhaps greatest when subject to noble rot, making some famous dessert wines like Sauternes and Barsac.

Thin-skinned grapes are prone to noble rot

WHITE BORDEAUX
Sémillon is the most important grape in the sweet and dry whites of Bordeaux.

ADAPTABLE SHIRAZ
In Australia, Shiraz is used to make sparkling and fortified wines, in addition to its world-famous still reds.

21 SYRAH (SHIRAZ)

Called Shiraz in Australia and South Africa, the Syrah grape makes dark, full-bodied, strong red wines with great potential longevity, particularly if oak-aged. Fairly tannic when young, these wines should reward keeping for at least three years; they are best with food. Mature Shiraz has aromas of blackcurrant, cedar, and mixed spice. Syrah is widely planted in the Rhône.

Vines are adaptable, thriving in warm places

WHITE ZINFANDEL
These black grapes also make "white" wine, called blush, which is usually very pale pink in color, light in body, and slightly sweet to the taste.

22 ZINFANDEL

Regarded as California's own grape variety, Zinfandel makes wines whose style can vary from light and elegant, as in the white or rosé wines, to massive and tannic reds, but the grape's intrinsic berrylike character always comes through. The best are arguably those that are rich and deeply colored, preferably with brief aging in oak. These will be at their peak after about five years.

Buds and ripens earlier than Cabernet sauvignon

23 OTHER IMPORTANT GRAPE VARIETIES

- Barbera makes light, fruity Italian reds.
- Colombard makes fresh, tangy white wines in France, California, and Australia.
- Müller-Thurgau is a mediocre relative of Riesling, used in cheap white German wine.
- Muscat covers several related white varieties, all with a distinctive musky aroma and grapey flavor. It is grown throughout southern Europe.
- Nebbiolo (red) is used for Italian Barolo.
- Pinot blanc and Pinot gris make whites in Italy, France, and Germany. Pinot blanc is similar to Chardonnay; Pinot gris is more aromatic.
- Sangiovese (red) is the main grape in Chianti.
- Sylvaner, a prolific grape, makes dry whites.
- Tempranillo (red) is the chief variety in Rioja.
- Viognier makes Condrieu, an excellent quality dry white that is perfumed and full-bodied.

△ CABERNET FRANC
Similar to (but not as good as) Cabernet sauvignon, it is always blended to make earthy, aromatic wines.

WHAT GRAPE?
Grape variety is by far the most important factor in influencing the style and flavor of a wine.

△ VARIETY: MUSCAT BLANC A PETITS GRAINS

VALUABLE VIOGNIER ▷
This grape is grown mainly in the Rhône valley. The yield can be unreliable, increasing the price of wine produced.

Slightly low acidity of grapes means wine is best drunk young

WHERE WINE IS PRODUCED

NORTH AMERICA

△ ENGLAND & WALES
Yields are as erratic as the climate, but medium grapey whites and a better drier style are characteristic.

Mexico has potential, but its grape crop is almost all distilled or used as table grapes

Israel's best wines (some of them kosher) are produced by the cooler vineyards of the Golan Heights

24 GROWTH INDUSTRY

Recent years have seen great changes in wine-making around the world. Divisions between the Old World, where tradition governed over science, and the more experimental New World, are disappearing as skill, expertise, technology, and investment are traded, and styles are imitated and invented with equal relish.

SOUTH AMERICA

Brazil's wines tend to be exported, while most wine from Uruguay is consumed locally

OLD WORLD–NEW WORLD
Europe and around the Mediterranean are called the Old World; the Americas, Australia, New Zealand, and South Africa are the New.

▽ MOLDOVA
Formerly part of the USSR, Moldova's wine industry is showing renewed potential.

▽ JAPAN
Wine produced here is often a blend of local and imported grapes.

△ TURKEY
Despite extremely large areas under vine, not much wine is made in this country where Islam – a religion that prohibits alcohol – dominates.

EUROPE

ASIA

AFRICA

China produces grape wine, but rice wine has long been more popular. This is changing with outside influence

India makes some decent sparkling wines using the Champagne method (Tip 53)

AUSTRALASIA

△ ZIMBABWE
The wine industry is young but expanding and improving.

△ GLOBAL WINE PRODUCTION
Both major and smaller areas are shown on the map in red.

25 WINE REGIONS OF FRANCE

Second only to Italy in quantity produced, the wines of France are role models the world over. Each of the main wine-producing regions has its own identity due to grape varieties, and local culture and climate. *Appellation contrôlée* laws in each area control the wine's origins and style.

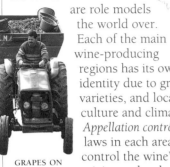

GRAPES ON
THE MOVE

26 ALSACE

The only region of France to have built its reputation on varietal wines (*Tip 77*), Alsace makes wines that are usually aromatic, dry, and full-bodied. Aside from Pinot noir, which makes light reds, all are white. The classic varieties are Gewürztraminer, Riesling, Muscat, and Pinot gris.

△ LATE GRAPE HARVEST
Thanks to warm sunshine and low rainfall, grapes can be harvested late; lusciously sweet wines are a local specialty.

△ PICTURESQUE RIQUEWIHR
This is one of many villages on the scenic Route du Vin, *which traverses the region.*

Alsatian wine master typifies the importance of tradition in this border region

27 BORDEAUX

This is the world's largest fine wine region. Some of its well-known districts are Médoc and Graves, where Cabernet sauvignon and Cabernet franc are the main varieties; Pomerol and St. Emilion, where Merlot dominates; and Sauternes, where fine sweet whites are made from Sauvignon blanc and Sémillon. Everyday wines are *petits châteaux*; fine wines are graded into five *crus classés* (classed growths), with *cru bourgeois* between the two.

△ BARRELS AT CHÂTEAU MARGAUX
Many fine red wines in Bordeaux are matured in oak barrels called barriques.

△ VINEYARD NEAR CHÂTEAU MARGAUX
The Médoc, one of Bordeaux's principal districts, is home to numerous world famous châteaux, among them Lafite, Latour, Margaux, and Mouton.

BORDEAUX WINES ▷
White wines tend to be a Sauvignon blanc and Sémillon blend. The reds are almost always blended – Merlot and Cabernet sauvignon in different ratios is most usual.

△ MECHANICAL HARVEST
Merlot grapes in St. Emilion are picked by machine – rather unusual for the area.

CLARET
This name for Bordeaux's reds (from the French claret, *"light red") remains as a legacy of when the region was ruled by the English more than 500 years ago.*

28 BURGUNDY

Stretching southward from near Dijon to Lyon, Burgundy includes the famous districts of Chablis, the Côte d'Or, Mâconnais, and Beaujolais. First of the French regions to achieve fame abroad, Burgundy still makes fine wine that is in great demand. The region is very fragmented, so classification is complex, and growers and merchants are important.

Traditional grape-picker's baskets now superseded by plastic

MÂCON VILLAGES   CÔTES DE BEAUNE

◁ FINE WINES
This region makes arguably the best Chardonnay (classic white Burgundy) and Pinot noir in the world, as well as the only top-notch Gamay wine.

△ CLOS DE VOUGEOT
This fine estate is made up of parcels owned and worked by over 85 growers.

29 LOIRE

White wines for early drinking dominate this region of generally good – rather than great – wine, so vintages are not crucial. Muscadet (dry, fruity whites), Saumur (sparkling Chenin blanc), Rosé d'Anjou, Pouilly Fumé (dry Sauvignon blanc), and Vouvray (Chenin blanc, sparkling and sweet) are well-known wines.

SANCERRE ▷
The area is famed for its good quality dry white wines.

WINE STYLES
White, sparkling, rosé, and red are all made here.

△ LOIRE GRAPES
Chenin blanc is the most important grape, followed by Sauvignon blanc and Muscadet. Red varieties are Gamay and Cabernet franc.

30 RHÔNE

This region divides neatly into two: the Syrah-dominated north and the Grenache-influenced south. The former makes expensive, spicy, full-bodied dark reds: Côte-Rôtie and Hermitage are celebrated names. The flatter south is more prolific, and wine quality can vary widely but usually offers good value. Châteauneuf-du-Pape, Côtes du Rhône, and Côtes du Rhône-Villages are noted appellations.

◁ RHÔNE WINE
Most is red, made from Syrah or Grenache grapes. Some white is made from secondary grape varieties.

△ HARVESTING SYRAH GRAPES
The steep difficult terrain in the upper reaches of Northern Rhône makes wine expensive to produce in Côte-Rôtie.

31 SOUTH OF FRANCE

Having for years been France's main source of cheap, plentiful drinking wines (*vins de table*), the wines from the south of France –

CELLAR SIGN
IN BANYULS

primarily Languedoc-Roussillon – have greatly improved. Today there is greater emphasis on better vines and use of modern technology, particularly from appellations like Fitou, Corbières, and Minervois.

△ CORBIÈRES
New technology and investment have greatly improved quality here.

◁ RED & WHITE
Languedoc makes quality wines like Corbières, as well as good value vins de pays. Provence makes red, rosé, and white wines.

CORBIÈRES   BANDOL

32 SPAIN & PORTUGAL

With a blend of tradition and innovation, Spain produces red, rosé, and white wines of varying quality. It is best known for Sherry (*Tip 56*), Rioja (oaky reds and whites), and sparkling Cava. Tempranillo and Garnacha (Grenache) are its most important grape varieties.

Aside from Port (*Tip 58*) and Madeira (*Tip 60*), Portugal makes red, white, and rosé wine. Since it joined the European Union, the quality of wine-making has improved a great deal.

△ VINEYARDS IN THE MINHO
This important Portuguese region makes Vinho Verde.

PORTUGUESE WINES ▷
Portugal uses grape varieties little grown elsewhere. Vinho Verde is a light white wine best drunk young. Dão's once coarse and tannic reds are now fruitier with spicy flavors.

◁ SPANISH BARRELS
American oak barrels are used in Rioja to age both reds and whites.

VINHO VERDE   DÃO

Cava is sparkling wine made using the Champagne method, and can be of excellent quality

WINES OF SPAIN ▷
Many wines are a blend of grapes. Red Rioja is typically a mix of Tempranillo and Garnacha, and white is mostly Viura (also known as Macabeo). Minor varieties abound.

△ ALAVESA DISTRICT, SPAIN
Wines from Rioja's three main districts, Alavesa, Alta, and Baja, are often blended.

33 ITALY

The largest wine-producing country in the world, Italy comprises many individualistic wine regions, each with its own local grapes and distinct style. Some fine wine is made, but the majority is modest; much of it is appropriate for drinking with local food. Bottle and label design are more innovative here than elsewhere in the world. Well-known Italian wines include Chianti (red in varying styles), Soave (dry but fruity white), and Marsala, Italy's fortified wine.

△ TUSCAN HARVEST
Sangiovese grapes are harvested for Chianti.

Dolcetto (an Italian equivalent of French Gamay) makes plump, juicy, early-drinking red wines

◁ ITALIAN WINES
Every imaginable style of wine is produced in Italy, but it is almost impossible to discern regional styles. In contrast to the very well-defined wine regions of France, vines of all varieties grow on all available plots of land.

CHIANTI CLASSICO   MOSCATO D'ASTI   VENEGAZZÙ DELLA CASA   DOLCETTO D'ALBA

PIEDMONT, NORTH ITALY ▷
Smoky, slow-maturing reds Barolo and Barbaresco hail from this region, as does sweet sparkling Asti.

CLASSIFICATION IN ITALY
Italy's appellation laws are being revised in order to standardize quality. Indicazioni Geografiche Tipiche, *an equivalent of the French* vin de pays, *has been introduced.*

34 GERMANY

Because Germany can be cool and damp during the growing season, grapes do not always ripen fully, resulting in high-acidity, low-alcohol white wines. The Rhine and the Mosel, a Rhine tributary, are the main wine regions. Totally dry wines can be rather sharp, but Riesling wines from *Kabinett* (*see below*) upward are Germany's great strength. On the crowded labels look for *Tafelwein* (modest table wine), *Landwein* (a dryish wine equal to French *vin de pays*), or *Qualitätswein*, which guarantees a minimum quality standard.

△ ROYAL SEAL
This sign marks the entry to a Rhineland vineyard.

▽ GERMAN WINES
Sweet Qualitätswein *is graded up from least-sweet* Kabinett, *to* Spätlese, Auslese, Beerenauslese, Eiswein (Tip 7), *to the sweetest, botrytized* (Tip 8) Trockenbeerenauslese.

Rhine bottles are always brown; Mosel are green

MOSEL
RIESLING

RHEINHESSEN
RIESLING

△ VINEYARDS ON THE MOSEL
South-facing slopes are best for giving ripening grapes the full benefit of the sun.

◁ SPRAYING PESTICIDES
Helicopters spraying vines epitomize the efficiency of the German wine industry.

35 REST OF EUROPE

Switzerland makes fresh, clean white wine, some uncomplicated Pinot noir and Gamay (red), and good Merlot (also red). Bulgarian wine, particularly Cabernet sauvignon (red), has vastly improved since the 1970s to cater to a large export market. Hungary, famous for sweet white Tokaji, Romania, and the Slovak Republic are trying to do the same, but entrenched wine-making traditions sometimes hinder progress.

△ WINES IN THEIR OWN RIGHT
Austria's wines can be sampled at Heurigen, where local growers are licensed to sell their own produce.

Labels may be traditional or in the modern style

AUSTRIAN CHARDONNAY   HUNGARIAN CABERNET SAUVIGNON

△ EUROPEAN WINES
Classic French varieties have long been cultivated, but each country has its indigenous varieties, too, such as Hungary's rich red Kadarka, Bulgaria's sturdy red Mavrud, and Romania's white Feteasca alba.

△ HUNGARIAN VINEYARDS
Mount Badacsony, an extinct volcano, provides a dramatic backdrop to the neat vineyards near Lake Balaton.

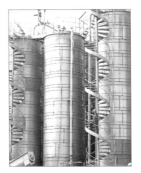
◁ FERMENTATION TANKS
Bulgaria's largest producer, Vini Sliven, exercises more control over wine-making by using new technology.

FOREIGN INVESTMENT
This enables modern technology to be used to monitor quality and wine-making practices.

36 NORTH AMERICA

Since the 1960s, North American wine has evolved and improved beyond recognition. Wine is produced across the continent, from both native grapes and exotic varieties, with wine-makers working in varied climatic conditions. California (*Tip 37*) is the most important region, but the Pacific Northwest (Oregon and Washington State), Atlantic Northeast (especially New York State and Virginia) make an important contribution, too. Canada's best wines are made around Lake Ontario.

WASHINGTON STATE ▷
Mechanical harvesters are widely used, as is irrigation, if needed.

▽ ONTARIO VINEYARD
Canadian wine is also produced in British Columbia, Nova Scotia, Alberta, and Quebec.

△ AMERICAN WINE
Traditional varieties, such as Pinot noir, Merlot, Riesling, and Chardonnay, are grown with varying success, but in colder areas – where growing seasons are short – other species predominate.

AVAs
Approved Viticultural Areas define region, not style or quality of wine.

▽ TRADITIONAL VARIETIES
Apart from California, Washington State grows the most classic varieties.

Newly harvested Sémillon grapes

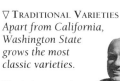

PACIFIC NORTHWEST

• San Francisco

CALIFORNIA

NEW YORK

ATLANTIC NORTHEAST

Midwestern states produce a small amount of wine, usually for the local trade

37 CALIFORNIA

Outside France, California – accounting for 95 percent of wine made in the United States – produces wines closest in style and quality to the great French wines. In this region of constant innovation and experimentation, climate is all-important. The coastal areas cooled by fog and wind, among them the Napa Valley and Sonoma, tend to make finer wine. The hot Central Valley, with its huge output of modest red "jug" wine, makes up the bulk of California's production.

Zinfandel makes many styles of wine: at best, rich, ripe, balanced reds

△ **RUSSIAN RIVER VALLEY**
Even a high-tech wine industry has a place for the humble milk carton.

◁ **SONOMA VALLEY**
This is a most prolific area of California, perhaps helped by the economical use of space.

CHARDONNAY ZINFANDEL

△ **CALIFORNIAN GRAPES**
Zinfandel, America's own grape, Chardonnay, and Cabernet sauvignon are the main varieties grown. Other important grapes include Merlot, Pinot noir, Syrah, Riesling, and Sauvignon blanc.

△ **NAPA VALLEY**
This is the heart of the Californian wine industry, with a deserved worldwide reputation for the fine wine it makes.

38 SOUTH AMERICA

Climatic conditions and inhospitable terrain preclude much of the continent from producing wine, but of the several countries that have healthy trades, Chile and Argentina are top producers. Chile enjoys a combination of ideal conditions, skilled wine-makers, and investment, and so produces some excellent red wines. Argentina, way ahead in quantity, uses bulk methods of production that do little to help it catch up in terms of quality.

△ TOO MUCH WATER
Flood irrigation gives high yields but poor-quality grapes.

◁ CHILEAN WINES
Fine red wines are made from Merlot, Cabernet sauvignon, and Pinot noir. Fine white wines are produced from Chardonnay, with greatly improving Sauvignon blanc and Riesling.

PHYLLOXERA-FREE ZONE
Vines are not grafted onto American rootstocks as else-where, because the vine louse (Tip 2) is not found in Chile.

△ CHILEAN WINE-MAKER
The progress of the grape crop is monitored on horseback.

Malbec gives spicy flavor to blend

ARGENTINA ▷
Malbec produces Argentina's best red wines, here with Cabernet sauvignon. Probably the best white is Torrontes. Chardonnay and Merlot are made, too.

△ VINEYARDS IN ARGENTINA
Mountain water is collected in winter from the Andes, then used for irrigation during the growing season.

39 SOUTH AFRICA

The Cape area, with its Mediterranean climate and diverse soils, produces most of the country's wines, which span the style spectrum from good dry whites to tannic reds, sparkling wine, and Port- and Sherry-style wines as well. The emphasis was once on quantity rather than quality, but South Africa is now reassessing its wine styles, making the reds softer and richer and some of its previously harsh whites fruitier.

△ NIGHT HARVEST
This is better for the grapes since it minimizes heat damage.

△ CONSTANTIA
Cape Dutch houses date local wine-making back to the mid-17th century.

△ BEAUTIFUL SCENERY
An arresting mountain landscape is typical of much of South Africa's wine-making region.

Chenin blanc, known locally as Steen, is the most planted grape

◁ GRAPE VARIETIES
The notable white varieties are Chenin blanc, Colombard, Chardonnay, and Sauvignon blanc. The native red variety, Pinotage, is joined by Merlot, Shiraz, and Cabernet sauvignon.

CHARDONNAY PINOTAGE CHENIN BLANC

NEW SOUTH AFRICA
During the isolation of the apartheid years, the wine industry developed along its own lines. It is now changing to come in line with international tastes.

40 AUSTRALIA

Fairly recent entries in the fine wine field, Australia now makes some of the most exciting wines in the world, in a huge range of styles and qualities. It has recently brought changes to the wine-making process that have been adopted worldwide, turning it into a high-tech industry. South Australia is the highest producer, but New South Wales, Victoria, and Western Australia contribute, too. New vineyards that capitalize on local conditions are being planted all the time. At present, no controlling appellation system exists.

△ REMONTAGE
Even in modern wineries, tasks like plunging the cap of grape skins – remontage – may be performed by hand.

△ BAROSSA VALLEY
Grape-pickers participate in the Vintage Opening Ceremony as harvest starts.

△ EDEN VALLEY, SOUTH AUSTRALIA
The Shiraz (Syrah) vines growing here are more than 100 years old.

SÉMILLON   SHIRAZ

◁ GRAPE VARIETIES
Shiraz (Syrah) and Cabernet sauvignon, often blended together, and Pinot noir dominate the reds. Successful whites are Sémillon, Chardonnay and Riesling.

MORE CONTROL
Australia was the pioneer of strict hygiene standards and tight control at all times, to keep the grape's own flavor in wines.

Style is dark, rich, and intensely sweet

◁ **FORTIFIED DELIGHT**
Liqueur Muscats and Tokay – not the same as Hungarian Tokaji (Tip 35) – have made a name for themselves as this country's premier fortified wines.

41 NEW ZEALAND

Since the early 1980s, this "new" wine-making country has revealed its fine potential. Talented wine-makers work well with the extremely variable climate, and are adventurous and innovative, using new techniques to produce well-balanced whites, some good reds, and fine sparkling wines from Chardonnay and Pinot noir. An appellation system is being planned.

GRAPE VARIETIES ▷
Sauvignon blanc to rival France's best Sancerre and Pouilly Fumé is produced, and also Chardonnay and Sémillon. Reds are made from Pinot noir, Merlot, and Cabernet sauvignon.

▽ **CENTRAL OTAGO**
Dramatic scenery typifies South Island vineyards, where the growing season is long and cool.

△ **PORT-STYLE**
Good Port-style wines are made from Grenache and Shiraz grapes in the Barossa Valley, South Australia.

◁ **CASK HALL**
Casks of aging wine at Rothbury Estate provide an evocative backdrop for dinners here.

HOW WINE IS MADE

42 HARVESTING GRAPES

Precisely when to pick the grapes is an agonizing decision for growers. As grapes ripen, their acid levels reduce, while sugar, color, and tannins increase. A wine's need for acidity must be balanced with the desire for richness gained from ripeness. Red wine benefits from riper grapes, but delaying harvest increases the risk of damage from rot, hail, and autumn frosts.

Shallow vessels stop grapes from being bruised

HARD WORK ▷
Harvesting by hand is slow and labor intensive, but does allow pickers to choose the best grapes.

43 WHY ARE GRAPES SOMETIMES DRIED?

Drying grapes reduces their water content, concentrating their sweetness in a similar way to noble rot (*Tip 8*). Historically, grapes were dried because the wines they made were more alcoholic, thus more stable and longer lasting. Italian Passito and French *vins de paille* continue the tradition today.

BAMBOO RACKS IN ITALY
Grapes are dried on racks, or hung up, for two to four weeks.

44 MAKING WHITE WINE

White wine is made from white grapes, although black grapes can be used if they are not crushed and are pressed immediately. After the juice has been allowed to "fall bright" – any sediment has settled – fermentation follows. This process is longer than for red wine (*Tip 45*), but exact temperature and duration vary with the style of wine made.

1 ◁ Grapes must be transported with care from the vineyard to winery as soon as possible after harvest, to make sure they stay in peak condition.

Machine removes stalks

2 ◁ Before the grapes are lightly crushed to release the juice and bring it into contact with yeasts on the grape skins, stalks, and seeds are removed.

3 ◁ The crushed grapes may be pumped into a tank called a Vinimatic to be macerated – steeped with their skins – for 12 to 48 hours to extract flavors and aromas stored in the skins.

Revolving tanks with fixed blade

4 ▷ Only juice that runs off (free-run) and that from the first pressing is fresh and fruity enough to be used for making white wine. This juice is allowed to fall bright and may also be filtered.

Extra yeast may be added to cleansed wine

△ PERSONAL SELECTION
Californian Chardonnay grapes are sorted into grades of quality; only the best can be used.

FERMENTATION CATALYSTS
Yeasts on the skins of ripe grapes convert fruit sugar into alcohol, turning grape juice into wine.

5 ◁ Fermentation takes place in either stainless-steel vats or in oak casks. Most white wines are filtered and bottled right away to preserve their freshness.

45 MAKING RED WINE

The process of making red wine is similar to that for making white. Its special feature is that the grape skins are kept in contact with the fermenting juice, giving much greater depth of flavor and color. Fermentation, lasting from 10 to 30 days, is at a higher temperature than for whites. Wine may be aged in casks or vats before bottling.

1 ◁ Red wine is almost always made from black grapes. Much of its character comes from tannins. These chemicals in the grape skins and seeds play a key role in aging red wine.

Stalks may be discarded before crushing

2 ◁ The stems and stalks are usually taken off: the tannins they contain are often too harsh. Grapes are then lightly crushed to release their juice, thus allowing fermentation to begin as quickly as possible.

3 ▷ Both juice and skins (at times even whole grape bunches) are put in a fermentation vat, where conditions are subject to very strict control. Grape solids give the juice color and tannins.

4 ▷ After fermentation on skins, free-run wine is drained off, and solids squeezed to release press-wine. A portion of this much more tannic liquid may be used at a later stage to balance the finished wine.

◁ SAMPLING WINE
A wine-maker in Burgundy carefully draws a sample from a barrel of maturing red wine to assess its progress.

5 ▷ Some inexpensive wine may be bottled right away, but most is run into oak casks or stainless-steel vats to age. Racking (running wine off sediment) and fining (clarifying wine) may be a part of the process.

Pipe to drain wine off its sediment

46 ROSÉ WINES

Rosés (simply "pink" wines) are most often made in the same way as reds (*Tip 45*), but the black grape skins are removed after only 12 to 36 hours. Blush wines – also pink – are made from black grapes that have been processed as if to make white wine (*Tip 44*). The two methods produce medium-dry and light, everyday wines, which are at their best drunk young and chilled.

MAKING PINK CHAMPAGNE
Adding a little red wine to the white blend produces this delicately pink Champagne.

47 THE TRADITION OF THE BARREL

Wooden barrels are still in popular use worldwide for making fine wines, despite their small size, and the time and effort needed to fill, empty, and clean them. The wood – usually oak – imparts tannins to the wine, which gives it a creamy vanilla character. Limited exposure to oxygen in the air through the pores in the wood helps to mature the wine.

Every aspect of barrel construction affects the taste of wine aged in it

STORING FULL BARRELS
In cellars, temperature and humidity can be controlled to produce ideal storage conditions.

48 MODERN TECHNOLOGY

Use of new technology has brought about greater control over all stages of wine-making, cutting production times, hence costs, greatly. Stainless steel has become very important: it is suited to rigorous temperature control and preserves wine's purity. Speeded-up stabilization processes enable the production of younger, fruitier, cheaper wine. Primarily thanks to Australian winemakers, strict hygiene is now a requirement.

SLEEK MODERN INDUSTRY
Less rustic than a traditional estate, the modern winery is, however, more efficient.

49 BOTTLING WINE

Although exact procedures vary, bottling usually takes place in a sterile environment and is fully automated. Aeration and agitation should be minimized, particularly for fine wine, so bottling equipment is both complex and expensive. Although most fine wine is bottled where it is made, modest wines may be bottled by a central agent.

WHEN TO BOTTLE?
Some wines are bottled as soon as they are made, but most fine wines are first aged in oak barrels or steel vats for some time.

ASSEMBLY LINE
Modern automated bottling equipment is designed to fill the bottles very gently, while letting in as little air as possible.

50 CORKS

Wine must be sealed to stop air from entering the bottle. Cork is the traditional stopper: it has no effect on the wine, is quite cheap to make, and is easy to remove. The longest and least-marked corks are of the finest quality, indicating good wine suitable for aging. Plastic and reconstituted corks are inexpensive alternatives, used on modest wines.

Made of compressed cork chips and dust

Hard to extract and does not age well

△ GENUINE CORKS
Wine corks are made from cork oak bark. Sheets are treated to kill bacteria, then the corks are stamped out.

SOLID CORK   RECONSTITUTED CORK   PLASTIC CORK

51 THE USE OF ADDITIVES

Sulfur dioxide (SO_2), a sulfite, may be added to control oxidation and kill unwanted bacteria. Many wines are clarified (fined), using agents such as egg white, gelatin, isinglass (protein from fish), liquid tannin, charcoal, and certain clays. Sorbic acid may be added to inhibit the growth of yeast and bacteria in sweet wines.

52 ORGANIC WINES

These are produced using only natural predators or herbicides in the vineyard, and a minimum of chemicals in wine-making. Current trends are to make wine as naturally as possible, which precludes the use of certain fining agents (*Tip 51*) and filtration techniques.

CRYSTALS
Sometimes found in fine wine, crystal deposits are harmless. Since preventing or removing them can wash out flavor, they're allowed to form.

SPARKLING WINE

53 THE CHAMPAGNE METHOD

The most famous sparkling wine is Champagne, named after its region of origin in France. What sets it apart is how it is made, a process of double fermentation that makes its tiny bubbles, or *mousse*. After the first simple fermentation, the wine is blended and bottled. Second fermentation follows, in these same bottles, once yeasts and sugars have been added; riddling (*see below*) and disgorgement (*see right*) are subsequent processes. The wine is then aged for one to three years.

◁ CHAMPAGNE VINEYARD
Grapes grown in this cool climate make acidic wines that form a good base for Champagne.

THREE MAIN GRAPES
Most Champagne is made from a blend of Chardonnay, Pinot noir, and Pinot meunier.

▽ RIDDLING, OR REMUAGE
After second fermentation, all the bottles are tilted from the horizontal to 90°, and twisted and shaken to move sediment into the neck.

When done by hand, riddling takes about eight weeks to complete

△ GYROPALETTE
Computerized machines that perform riddling are less labor intensive: the process is completed in only eight days.

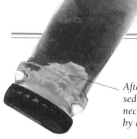

After riddling, the sediment in the neck is removed by disgorgement

DISGORGEMENT, OR DÉGORGEMENT
The plug of sediment is removed by passing the neck through a freezing solution. When the cap is removed, the sediment is forced out by internal pressure. The bottle may be topped off with a dosage of wine and sugar.

FLAVOR DEVELOPS WITH AGING
After second fermentation, the Champagne is aged in the bottles in which it will be sold for at least a year, but often much longer.

54 CHAMPAGNE BOTTLE NAMES

From the smallest up, Champagne (and sometimes other wine) bottles are known as Quarter; Half; Bottle; Magnum (2 bottles); Jeroboam (4 bottles); Rehoboam (6 bottles, but no longer made); Methuselah (8 bottles); Salmanazar (12 bottles); Balthazar (16 bottles); and the giant Nebuchadnezzar (20 bottles).

Jeroboam holds 4 standard bottles

CHAMPAGNE BOTTLE SIZES

55 OTHER WAYS TO ADD BUBBLES

Besides the Champagne region, many other areas make sparkling wine. The Champagne method may be used, but other methods are more common and cheaper:
- transfer method: following second fermentation in bottles, sediment is filtered under pressure in a vat, after which the wine is rebottled.
- charmat or tank method: second fermentation takes place in a tank, rather than in individual bottles.
- carbonation: the cheapest method whereby wine is injected with CO_2.

FORTIFIED WINE

56 HOW SHERRY IS MADE

Fortified wine is made by adding neutral grape spirit to a wine base. To make Sherry, the spirit is added once fermentation has stopped. The hot climate and unusual soil in Jerez de la Frontera, southern Spain, is uniquely suited to producing the base wine from which Sherry is made. The type is determined by assessing the wine regularly to see how best to develop it. Once the style is set, the wine matures in a *solera* (a blending system), to keep quality constant.

△ ALBARIZA SOIL
Vines growing on this unique chalky soil produce grapes with a higher acidity than you would expect for so hot a climate.

△ COLLECTING SUN-DRIED GRAPES
Pedro Ximenez grapes are the traditional sweetening agent for Sherry. They are left to dry in the sun to concentrate the sugars.

A venencia is used to penetrate the froth of flor in sherry casks

JEREZ TO SHERRY
Sherry derives from Jerez, the area where it is made.

△ BODEGA ENTRANCE
Wineries making Sherry in Jerez are called bodegas. Many are open to the public.

Palomino grape is classic Sherry variety

Press designed so seeds are not split in drum

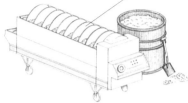

1 △ Grapes are de-stalked, seeded, and pressed in cylindrical stainless-steel presses. This is usually done at night, to minimize the effect of heat from the sun.

2 ◁ Fermentation takes place in stainless-steel vats. After fermentation the alcohol level is around 11 percent, and the wine completely dry; any sweetness required is added later.

3 ▷ Fortification – the addition of pure grape spirit – takes place after fermentation, raising the alcohol level to 15.5–18 percent.

4 ◁ To keep quality constant, younger wine in the top barrels (*soleras*), is mixed with old wine below. Bottling is from the bottom, oldest *solera*.

57 STYLES OF SHERRY

A unique yeast derivative, *flor*, may appear in some barrels but not others. Where it does, crisp, dry Fino and Manzanilla (Fino from a particular area) result. The fuller-styled Amontillado has little *flor* character but is aged without it. Oloroso, rich and nutty, has none.

MANZANILLA   FINO   AMONTILLADO

◁ WHAT IS IT? *Pure Sherry is always dry, but the wine may then be sweetened to varying degrees.*

DECANTING *Sherry of any style need not be decanted.*

OLOROSO   CREAM

58 WHAT IS PORT?

Port is a sweet, fruity, full-bodied fortified wine. It originated in the Douro in northern Portugal, where it is made from numerous local grape varieties. Grape spirit is added before the end of fermentation. Sugars, left unfermented, account for Port's sweetness. Drier styles have a longer fermentation, and less spirit is added. Several other places like Australia, South Africa, and California now also make Port-style wines.

△ PEOPLE POWER
Some small producers still tread the grapes manually.

▽ SCIENCE OF BLENDING
Port is made and fortified in the Douro, but blending and bottling is usually done near Oporto.

VINEYARDS WHEREVER POSSIBLE
Terracing has long been used to maximize use of the land. Wider terraces now accommodate mechanization.

59 MAJOR STYLES OF PORT

The main variations in style result from the aging process. Both ruby and tawny are wood aged; ruby is drunk young. Tawny describes many styles, the finest being 10, 20, and over 30 years old. Vintage, only produced in good years, is aged in bottles for at least ten years.

TAWNY   RUBY   VINTAGE

60 MADEIRA

Named after the island where it is made, Madeira, like Port, is fortified during fermentation. It has a special baked flavor, achieved by a process called *estufagem*, which heats the wine in ovens, then cools it down. Four types exist, originally identified by the grape varieties used: Sercial (light and dry), Verdelho (medium dry), Bual (medium sweet), and Malmsey (richest and sweetest).

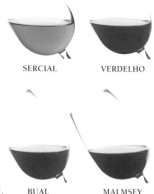

SERCIAL

VERDELHO

BUAL

MALMSEY

BARREL END, MADEIRA

DESSERT WINES
Australia produces the best Liqueur Muscats and Tokays, but other countries such as France also make fine examples.

French Muscat is light in color

61 LIQUEUR MUSCATS & TOKAYS

These dessert wines are very sweet. The grapes – Muscat and Muscadelle (called Tokay in Australia) – are picked late to maximize sweetness. The wine is fortified with grape spirit before the end of fermentation, and then wood-aged using a combination of the *solera* system (*Tip 56*), and *estufagem* (*Tip 60*).

62 AROMATIZED WINES

Fortified wines that have aromatic ingredients (usually herbs and spices) added are known as aromatized wines. Vermouth, the best known, traditionally has wormwood added and can be many different styles and qualities. Red is sweet, white is dry or sweet.

Wermut, *the German word for the herb wormwood, gave vermouth its name*

BRAND NAMES
Most aromatized wines are made and sold under recognizable brand names, like Cinzano and Martini.

ASSESSING WINE

63 TASTING DO'S AND DON'TS

Formal tastings should take place in a neutral, well-lit environment. Use your senses of sight, smell, and taste, in that order, to assess and evaluate a wine.

- Do clear your palate with water between wines.
- Do make notes of your impressions of all wines.
- Don't eat anything before or during a tasting.
- Don't wear perfumes: aromas are intrusive.

KEEP IT SIMPLE
If you host a tasting, stick to one region or style so comparisons are more meaningful.

CONCEAL ANY CLUES ▷
Cover all wine labels so that you cannot be influenced by information on them. Use glasses with wide bowls and narrow mouths to concentrate aromas. Fill one-third at most.

64 WHAT DOES THE COLOR SHOW?

Hue, intensity, and depth of color, especially in red wines, can give an indication of grape varieties used, and maturity and age of the wine. Clarity is significant, too: a young wine will be brighter than an old one. Cloudiness may be just disturbed sediment but can signify a fault. Study wine in natural light, since artificial light affects its color.

65 VISCOSITY

Further insights into the nature of a wine you are tasting can be gained from its viscosity, seen in "legs" or "tears" that cling to the side of the glass after the wine has been swirled around. If prominent traces are left, the wine has a high alcohol or sugar content, or both.

OBVIOUS TEAR
This wine is likely to have a high alcohol content.

DIRTY DECOY
Clean all traces of detergent and dirt off glasses.

66 LOOKING AT WHITE WINES

White wines range from a colorless, water-white to a deep gold color, but most are a light straw yellow, darkening with age. In general, paler-colored wines come from cooler regions, darker wines from warm areas. Exceptions are the very sweet wines, notably botrytized (*Tip 8*) and oak-aged whites, which are a deeper color. Young whites may be tinged green, and a brownish wine could be off.

Defined edge, in spite of watery color, suggests wine of quality

Pale color may indicate cool climate

◁ **WATER WHITE**
The aroma and taste of the wine will help dismiss other options, such as Portuguese Vinho Verde, suggested by the bubbles, and confirm this to be Riesling.

Abundant bubbles show that wine is sparkling

Color is clear and bright

◁ **LEMON YELLOW**
Sniffing will reveal the grape variety to be Chardonnay, while tasting (and feeling the bubbles) provides clues as to whether it is Champagne.

Color doesn't fade at rim

Color could be indicative of age or sweetness

◁ **YELLOW GOLD**
Any misleading visual clues are discounted immediately once Gewürztraminer's distinct aroma is picked up.

Old gold color immediately suggests fullness and richness

Intense color correctly implies sweetness

◁ **OLD GOLD**
The aroma reveals it is botrytized, and tasting confirms the presence of Sémillon's classic honeyed flavors.

67 LOOKING AT RED WINES

The color of red wine, pink to almost black, is largely due to the grape variety, but factors like age and region of origin also play a part. In contrast to whites, reds lighten with age: the browner and paler the rim (best observed by tilting the glass away from you) the more mature the wine. Warm areas usually produce darker-colored wines, while oak-aged wines lose more color than bottle-aged ones.

Color fades toward the rim, so wine is likely to be of medium quality

Orange tint suggesting Pinot noir or Grenache

◁ **LIGHT ORANGE**
Perfumed aroma and strawberry fruit with no pepperiness (typical of the Grenache grape) confirms the variety must be Pinot noir.

Brick-red color and a watery edge – may suggest Bordeaux

No sign of brown (thus age) in color

◁ **BRICK RED**
On tasting, the wine reveals a firm palate, but one that is not rich and capable of aging: so the wine is a modest Bordeaux red.

Purple rim suggests minor quality Syrah in Beaujolais

Color is clear and well defined

◁ **CLEAR GARNET**
The wine has the peardrop aroma associated with Beaujolais, so the grape variety must be Gamay.

Intense color gives clues to hot climate

Black color is nearly opaque

◁ **ALMOST BLACK**
The spicy aroma is that of the Syrah grape: it's probably a Rhône – there's no sign of New World vanilla oak.

68 USING YOUR SENSE OF SMELL

A wine's aroma can reveal a lot about its condition and character. To assess the "nose" of a wine, swirl it around in the glass and take a deep sniff: your first impressions are crucial. Does it smell fresh? How intense is the aroma? Does it remind you of anything? (*Tip 70* describes common associations.)

GRAPEY AROMA?
Although wine may smell fruity, it does not often smell of grapes.

NOSE TEST
A Burgundy wine-maker monitors the progress of aging wine by nosing it.

Important sensors are in upper part of nose

Smells enter nose in form of vapor

69 TASTING

Take a reasonable mouthful of wine, but resist the urge to swallow it. Roll it around your mouth instead, exposing it to all your taste-buds. Breathe in over it, since this further releases all its flavors. Try to assess the strength of alcohol, and the acidity and sweetness.

Back and top of tongue recognize bitterness, perhaps from tannins

Sides of tongue detect sharpness and acidity

Tongue's tip registers sweetness

70 FLAVORS OF WINE

Many seemingly improbable descriptions of the aroma or taste of wine actually have a scientific basis: identical chemical compounds are found in certain wines and the items with which they are compared. Do not worry if these associations don't suggest themselves to you: they are meant simply as handles to build your experience and heighten your pleasure in drinking wine.

Other common associations are: gas and mature Riesling; coffee and mature Champagne; spices and oak-aged red wines; and blackcurrants and Cabernet sauvignon.

◁ *Banana and pear aromas can show that the wine was fermented at a low temperature, which is common for Beaujolais and inexpensive whites.*

△ *Black pepper is an aroma often evoked by spicy reds from the Syrah grape.*

△ *Toast can be a sign of new oak barrels, or bottle-aged Chardonnay or Sémillon.*

△ *Peach and apricot suggest New World Chardonnay (as does pineapple), ripe Riesling, or Muscat.*

△ *Honeyed flavors emerge in mature dessert wines or where grapes were subject to noble rot.*

△ *Nutty overtones, hazelnut or walnut, mean the wine is likely to be mature white Burgundy.*

△ *Green pepper implies inexpensive young reds from Cabernet sauvignon or Cabernet franc.*

△ *Lime or lemon flavors are often found in wines made from Sémillon and Australian Riesling.*

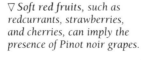
▽ *Soft red fruits, such as redcurrants, strawberries, and cherries, can imply the presence of Pinot noir grapes.*

△ *Chocolate may characterize a fine full-bodied red wine: ripe, mature, and low in acidity.*

△ **Vanilla** is often associated with wine that has been aged in new oak.

△ **Raspberry** flavors emerge in inexpensive red Rhônes, often from Syrah grapes.

△ **Litchis** are very strongly evoked when nosing a Gewürztraminer wine in any style.

△ **Rose petals** are a more subtle sign of Gewürztraminer than lychees (left), but may be Muscat.

△ **Butter** means Chardonnay of all styles: both Old and New World.

△ **Gooseberries** imply Sauvignon blanc is the grape variety used.

▽ **Mint and eucalyptus** are both indicative of Cabernet sauvignon, usually from Australia, South Africa, or California.

71 BALANCE, WEIGHT, & BODY

Ideally, acid, alcohol, fruit, and tannins should be balanced. Not enough acidity makes a wine dull (flat and short); equally too much makes it sharp and raw. An excess of tannins makes a wine bitter, but the right amount of both acidity and tannins means the fruit is refreshing and the flavor lingers. Balance can alter with time.

Weight refers to alcohol content, and body refers to the mixture of fruitiness and alcohol: the "feel" of it in your mouth. Full-bodied wine is alcoholic and fruity; light wine is crisp, with a low alcohol content.

72 WHAT IS MEANT BY LENGTH

Wines where the flavor lingers in the mouth after swallowing are called long, and this is considered to be a positive description: the intensity and persistence of flavor reflect the quality of the wine. The aroma and flavor continuing in the mouth after the wine has been swallowed is called its aftertaste: the quality and enjoyment of a wine's aftertaste, combined with how long it lingers, is described as its finish. The finish can sometimes give an indication of how a wine might age: poor wine invariably produces an unexciting end.

BOTTLES & LABELS

73 ANATOMY OF THE BOTTLE

Until the 17th century, wine was stored in vessels of stoneware or pottery. Glass then became the material of choice as technology in its making and shaping advanced. Early wine bottles were rounded.

The shape was streamlined when it was discovered that wine improved with laying down. Now, a heavier glass tends to signify quality wine, and irregular sizes and shapes are used to make design statements.

Capsule or foil, made of tin or plastic

Space between wine and cork is called ullage

Slope of shoulder varies with bottle style

Neck label is not always present

Style of front label varies regionally and from one producer to another

Back label is optional, but often useful

BOTTLE SIZE ▷
Although shapes differ, standard wine bottles all have a capacity of 750ml/75cl.

Punt is most important for sparkling wine

△ PACKING WINE BOTTLES
Bottles are cased carefully in boxes, with protective packaging to guard against breakages.

PUNT MEANS QUALITY?
A punt (indentation at the base of some bottles) doesn't affect the wine, but indicates that it is expected to be laid down to age.

74 BOTTLE SHAPES & COLORS

Individual designs are becoming popular, yet the greatest influence on bottle shape and color is still the region from which it comes and the style of wine in it. The two most common styles are the classic Burgundy and Bordeaux shapes (*see right*). If they are used, it tends to suggest the wine's style – red or white – is similar to that of a classic Bordeaux or Burgundy, giving you extra clues about the contents.

Slender bottle, with no punt

△ **German** wine bottles are tall and thin. The green or brown bottles are only for white wine.

Dark to pale green with high shoulders

△ **Bordeaux** wine bottles are often used for red wines that will have to be laid down to age.

Short and slightly squat, with punt

△ **Burgundy** wine bottles are used for both red and white wines in regions all over the world.

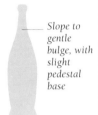

Slope to gentle bulge, with slight pedestal base

△ **Provençal** wine bottles are used throughout the region for white, red, and rosé wines.

Clear glass is best for showing off the wine's color

△ BOTTLE COLORS
Wine keeps best in dark-colored bottles, but it is a mix of tradition and producer's choice that determines what color is used.

Cork is wired on due to internal pressure

△ **Sparkling** wine bottles are made of thick glass, with a high punt to increase inside surface area.

Typical bulbous neck

△ **Port** bottles are dark brown, with definite shoulders and a longish neck for a full cork.

75 READING A WINE LABEL

Regions differ in what the law requires them to include on labels, but the trend worldwide is toward giving more information. The most important thing to look for is: what sort of wine is it? Where does it come from? Is the style of wine or grape variety given? Is there an indication of quality in the form of an appellation grading? Its age, shown by the vintage, is important to determine if it is ready to drink.

FRENCH LABELS ▷
Grape varieties are seldom given on labels. AOC (Appellation d'Origine Contrôlée) usually signifies a wine of good quality.

Official regional grading reveals a quality wine

Picture of estate: expect some artistic license

VISUAL IMPACT
Don't expect the label to be any reflection on the quality of wine in the bottle.

GRAND CRU CLASSÉ EN 1855

Name of property where wine was made

CHATEAU SAINT-PIERRE
1986
SAINT-JULIEN
APPELLATION SAINT-JULIEN CONTRÔLÉE

Wine bottled on estate where made

MIS EN BOUTEILLES
AU CHATEAU

NEC PLURIBUS
IMPAR

DOMAINES HENRI MARTIN
PROPRIÉTAIRE À SAINT-JULIEN-BEYCHEVELLE, GIRONDE 33250
PRODUCE OF FRANCE

75cl

Vintage indicates year of harvest

Capacity is 750ml: standard bottle size worldwide

Alcoholic strength (shown as percent of volume)

Area where property is located

Name of official appellation of area

Official grading shows wine is of high quality

Name of region where wine was made

Name of wine (here also name of estate)

Riserva means wine has been aged for a set number of years

RHEINPFALZ

1988er
DEIDESHEIMER MAUSHÖHLE
RIESLING AUSLESE

Name of town, followed by vineyard

Grape variety and its level of sweetness

CASTELLO DEI RAMPOLLA

RISERVA 1985
CHIANTI CLASSICO
75cl

Classico is best part of any quality zone

Name of proprietor is often given

△ **GERMAN LABELS**
QmP, Qualitätswein mit Prädikat, *is the top quality, then* QbA, Qualitätswein bestimmter Anbaugebiete, Landwein, *and* Tafelwein.

△ **ITALIAN LABELS**
Denominazione di Origine Controllata e Garantita, DOCG, *is the top quality, then* DOC. VT, Vino da Tavola *is table wine.*

Appellation gives region (Rioja), then quality (DO)

Label states wine is white; may also specify style

Stamp of regulator guarantees wine

△ SPANISH LABELS
Denominacion de Origen Calificada, *DOCA*, is the top quality, then *DO*, Denominacion de Origen. Vino de Mesa, *VdM*, is table wine.

Name of region and vineyard usually appear

Grape varieties are always given, unless wine is a blend

△ NEW WORLD LABELS
Not all countries have their own appellation system, but wine labels often provide useful details about grapes and wine style. Generic names like Chablis can be misused.

Quinta indicates wine is from single vineyard or estate

Style (tawny, ruby, or vintage) and if it is aged are specified

Name of producer

△ PORT LABELS
No appellation system exists for Port, but style and age (10-, 20-, 30-, or Over 40-Year-Old) usually appear on the label.

76 THE BACK LABEL

Always read the back label if there is one, since it may contain a fuller description of the wine (and its style and origin) than is revealed by the front and neck labels. Some information required by law – for example, the alcohol content per volume – may also appear on the back. Importers and distributors frequently print customized back labels for particular markets.

77 VARIETALS & BLENDS

Varietal wines are made from one grape variety; a blend is a mix of two or more. Neither style is inherently superior, since grape quality and wine-making are still far too influential. Old World wines used to be blends, and New World were varietals, but this is no longer always the case.

Tasting throughout aging is vital for blending

BUYING WINE

78 PURCHASING FROM A RETAILER

Whether you buy wine from a liquor outlet or a supermarket, always ask questions (*Tip 81*), and take advantage of any tastings and special offers so that you can sample as many different styles as possible. To assist customers, many stores (supermarkets in particular) have devised classification systems that are particularly useful if labels do not give enough information.

ORDERED SELECTION
Refer to any guidelines the store may give to help find the style of wine you like.

79 BUYING WINE WHERE IT IS MADE

The principal advantage of buying wines direct from the grower is the opportunity to find out all about the wines at their source and often taste them before you buy. Visiting small producers can be particularly exciting since their wines may have a limited area of distribution. Some producers serve food and offer informative guided tours as well.

BARGAIN BASEMENT?
Taste before you buy, but don't expect wine bought direct from the producer to be cheaper than that from retail outlets.

TAKING A CLOSER LOOK
When visiting a winery, you may be able to observe parts of the wine-making process.

80 INFLUENCE OF THE WINE-MAKER

Neighboring wine-makers using the same grape variety and similar technology may produce different wines, proving the human element can never be overlooked. Growers play a vital role, too, making crucial decisions each season. "Flying wine-makers" capitalize on the opposite seasons in the two hemispheres, applying their skills internationally.

ACQUIRED SKILL OR INBORN TALENT?
It is almost impossible to pinpoint exactly what it is that creates a good wine-maker.

81 WHAT TO ASK WHEN YOU BUY WINE

It is worth asking questions like these to maximize your enjoyment of the wine you're buying:
- What is the ideal age to drink it?
- Which grape variety is it made from (if not shown on the label)?
- How long will the wine keep?
- Will it need to be decanted?
- Should it be chilled?
- Will the glass shape affect taste?
- What foods complement/detract from it – or is it best drunk alone?

82 INVESTING IN WINE

The theory behind investing in wine is that its value increases as it matures. In practice, wine as an investment is risky, due to all the variables involved. Skill, knowledge, timing, and luck are all essential, so try to learn as much as possible to prevent costly mistakes. Remember that wine should always be drunk for enjoyment and appreciation.

Think before bidding if you are new to wine and auctions

A UNIQUE ARCHIVE ▷
Old vintages, such as these of Château Margaux, are very valuable. They need to be stored in cool bottle cellars.

STORING WINE

83 WHERE TO STORE YOUR WINE

A naturally constant environment is the crucial storage consideration. Fluctuations in temperature can be harmful (*Tip 85*), as can too much movement (including vibrations) and very low humidity. Undesirable photochemical effects of sunlight and artificial light are reversed once darkness is restored. Renting professional cellar space is a good option if your interest warrants it.

84 THE CORRECT ANGLE TO STORE

Wine bottles should be stored horizontally and cases stacked on their sides, ensuring that the corks remain moist, thus fully swollen and airtight. If a bottle is stored vertically, its cork eventually dries out and shrinks. This exposes the wine to air and causes it to oxidize and go off. A few hours prior to drinking, stand the bottle upright to allow any sediment to settle.

UNDISTURBED RESTING PLACE
Underground cellars are usually cool, damp, dark, and secure, making them the ideal place for storing stocks of fine wine.

CUSTOM-MADE WINE RACKS
Most wine racks allow you to store bottles horizontally. Protecting them from light as well, as this one does, is also advisable.

85 THE CORRECT STORAGE TEMPERATURE

The optimum temperature for storing wine is 52°F (11°C), but anywhere from 40°F to 65°F (5°C to 18°C) will do no harm, as long as there is little short-term fluctuation: erratic temperatures are the most dangerous. Wine matures faster at higher temperatures and slower when they are low.

HIGH RISE
When storing wine, remember that heat rises.

Constant temperature is important

86 HOW LONG TO KEEP WINE

Wine is "ready to drink" for some time: exact timing is a trade-off between freshness and mellowness.
- Very old wines are safe to drink.
- White grapes that age well include Chardonnay, Riesling, and Sémillon.

- Cabernet sauvignon, Zinfandel, Merlot, and Syrah (Shiraz) are red varieties that benefit from aging.
- Many modest wines are made to drink on purchase; whites within six months, reds within two years.

87 STORING WINE IN A REFRIGERATOR

Placing a bottle of wine in the refrigerator to chill for a few hours is fine: leaving it there any longer can cause the cork to stick. The refrigerator draws moisture from the cork, which increases the possibility of oxidation. Immersing a bottle in a bucket of ice and water is the best way to cool wine and to keep it cool while drinking.

ROOM TEMPERATURE REDS
Take the chill off everyday red wines by placing them, unopened (capsule removed), in the microwave at half power for 60–90 seconds.

A brief spell in the freezer works well in an emergency

Standing bottles upright allows any sediment to settle

PREPARING WINE

88 WHICH GLASS?

Whether you are tasting or drinking purely for enjoyment, the ideal vessel for any wine is one with a bulbous base and inwardly sloping sides. This concentrates the aromas in the top of the glass, giving you full benefit of a wine's bouquet. Fill the glass only to a half to two-thirds, so that aromas can circulate. Colorless glass shows off the wine's color, and a stem allows you to swirl the wine more easily without affecting the wine's temperature.

WHAT SHAPE TO CHOOSE
Choose a style you like, where the bowl is large enough and wider than the rim.

89 CARE OF WINE GLASSES

LINT-FREE CLOTH

Wash and dry glasses immediately after use with a mild detergent. Always rinse glasses thoroughly in hot water before drying with a clean cloth. Store glasses upright, so as not to trap stale air in the bowls.

90 SERVE AT THE CORRECT TEMPERATURE

Follow the guidelines below to be sure of enjoying wine to the fullest.
- Sparkling: 40–45°F (4.5–7°C).
- Whites: 45–50°F (7–10°C).
- Reds: rosés and light reds: 50–55°F (10–12.5°C); medium-bodied: 55–60°F (12.5–15.5°C); full-bodied: 60–65°F (15.5–18°C).

Ice in cold water chills wine effectively and keeps it cold

AVOID EXTREMES
Overchilling kills the flavor and aroma. Too much warmth makes wine taste bland.

91 WITHDRAWING THE CORK

The most efficient corkscrew is one that has an easy-to-grip handle and a rounded open spiral; those with a solid core and sharp edges do not grip well, boring a hole through the cork instead. Before extracting the cork, carefully remove the foil covering it, and wipe around the neck to clean it.

Easy-to-grip wooden handle

Screw is well rounded with no sharp edges

◁ CORK PULLER

◁ FOIL CUTTER
Use to slice the capsule or foil top, exposing the cork ready to extract.

Cutting wheels are protected

▽ CORK EXTRACTOR

Use to replace cork, if necessary

△ SCREWPULL®

92 EXTRACTING A BROKEN WINE CORK

A cork that has crumbled, or is very tightly compacted, is best removed by inserting the corkscrew at an angle, since this offers good leverage. Move the bottle as gently as possible.

Small blade, used for slicing off capsule

△ WAITER'S FRIEND
Positioned properly on the rim, the folding arm gives extra leverage. If wrongly used, it may break the rim.

1 Insert the corkscrew diagonally across the cork. Pull smoothly, trying to keep the bottle as steady as possible.

2 Pry the cork out carefully, keeping the angle and being careful not to allow any crumbs to fall into the bottle.

FLOATING CORK CHIPS
Bits of cork floating in wine are almost always harmless and seldom indicate a fault. Remove, and taste to confirm that the wine is not off.

Pour slowly, allowing any frothy bubbles to dissipate

93 OPENING A BOTTLE OF SPARKLING WINE

Great care must be taken when opening a bottle of sparkling wine, because the contents are under such high pressure. Aim it away from other people (and anything breakable) since the cork could shoot off. Always hold the bottle with a cloth napkin in case it breaks. If the cork is particularly sticky, run the neck under warm water to increase the pressure.

1 After removing the foil, untwine and take off the wire. Have a napkin ready for Step 2, since the cork may shoot off.

2 Rather than turning the cork around, twist the bottle away from you, so that the top of the cork does not break off.

3 Once the cork is out, quickly cover the top with your hand to slow the release of pressure and stem any overflow.

94 DO WINES NEED TO BREATHE?

Exposing young, tannic, full-bodied red wine to air before you drink it can develop its aromas and soften its flavors, but most other wine will not benefit from breathing. Do open the bottle about half an hour before you want to drink it, to allow bottle stink – the harmless stale-smelling air trapped between the wine and the cork – to dissipate.

95 HOW TO TELL IF A WINE IS OFF

If an unpleasant smell remains or worsens after the bottle is opened, the wine may be off: if it tastes like vinegar, or has a flat, Sherrylike flavor, there is probably a fault. Cork bark can occasionally become infected, contaminating stoppered wines and making them taste musty, woody (the true meaning of the term "corked"), and unpalatable.

96 DECANTING WINE

With increasing age, many wines, especially reds, throw a deposit of tannins and color pigments. To remove this, the wine needs to be decanted: poured off its sediment. Stand the bottle upright several hours before you start, to allow the sediment to collect. Gently remove the cork and wipe round the neck to clean it, inside and out. Decant the whole bottle in one movement.

△ KEEP A STEADY HAND
Pour wine carefully but steadily (try not to let it glug) directly over a light source like a candle or flashlight. This will reveal any sediment as you near the end of the bottle.

FILTER PAPER ▷
Pour the dregs of your decanted wine gently through fine coffee filter paper.

DO NOT DISTURB
Keep agitation to a minimum, since it disturbs sediment.

97 HOW LONG WILL WINE STAY FRESH?

Air acts on wine from the moment the bottle is opened, and although it will not spoil (oxidize) for several days, wine is at its best and freshest when it is first opened. If you know you can't finish wine in one sitting, recork and refrigerate it as soon as possible. White wines should last around two days, reds for three to four, although both will taste a little flatter for having been open.

STOP THE BOTTLE
When it is not possible to finish wine at one sitting, prevent air from getting in by using a completely airtight stopper, such as these.

△ STOPPERS
SUITABLE FOR
STILL WINE

△ SPARKLING WINE
STOPPER

VACU-VIN® ▷
This creates a vacuum in the bottle: good for taking unwanted bubbles out of inexpensive red wines, but not so good for the aromas of more delicate wines.

*Rubber ____
stopper can
be reused*

ENJOYING WINE

98 WINE WITH FOOD

Balance is the key: food and wine need to complement, never overpower, each other. Neutral food is best with fine wine. Seek advice on foods that are difficult to match, such as chocolate, strong cheeses, grapefruit, asparagus, and pickles. Where possible, team regional food with its local wines. Allow personal preference to be your main guide.

Consider other ingredients, too

Bitter leaves need acidic wine

△ DRESSED SALADS
If there is lemon or vinegar in the dressing, wine should be acidic to balance it. Light, dry whites, more acidic than reds, suit salads. Sauvignon blanc is a good choice.

△ MADE WITH EGGS
The effervescence of sparkling wine is the perfect foil to the soft texture of egg dishes, while at the same time not drowning out eggs' somewhat subtle flavor.

FISH DISHES ▷
The sauce fish is cooked in or served with makes all the difference: creamy sauces need high acidity and effervescence, so choose dry whites – although fish cooked in red wine will taste good with red wine. Oak-aged Chardonnay is a good match for smoked fish.

VEGETARIAN WINE
Animal products such as isinglass (from fish) and gelatin (from beef) may be used as fining agents to clarify wine, but are usually avoided in the making of vegetarian wine. Remember, it may not be organic (Tip 52).

Wine style determined by sauce

△ RICH & CREAMY
Medium to full-bodied whites best match the creaminess of rich sauces. The buttery flavor of Chardonnay particularly complements buttery sauces. Avoid very fruity wines.

△ HEARTY FARE
If you observe the golden rule on balance, this heavy meal must be teamed with an equally weighty red: a full-bodied, tannic wine such as Cabernet sauvignon is ideal.

DESSERTS ▷
Sweets usually taste unpleasant with very dry wine. Dessert wines are the obvious choice, but some argue that they're best enjoyed alone. Just decide for yourself.

Flavorful hard cheeses need full rich wines

△ HOT & SPICY
Ice-cold beer is a better match than wine for really spicy food. If you do want wine, though, sweetness sometimes proves a good contrast to spices: try a Gewürztraminer.

FRESH FRUIT ▷
Fruits that are high in acid can make wines taste metallic and thin. In general, drink sweet whites, especially botrytized, late-harvest, or sparkling.

△ CHEESE BOARD
Sweet wine, especially Port, complements blue cheeses. Avoid heavy reds with soft cheeses. Very strong cheeses can overwhelm any wine.

99 DRINKING ORDER

Try to ascend in quality and flavor, but do consider what food you are serving if the wine is to accompany a meal (*Tip 98*).

- Serve cheap before expensive: a step back in quality is noticeable.
- Drink dry before sweet: sweet wines make dry taste very acidic.
- Light wines come before full-bodied: weighty and fortified wines will overpower a lighter wine.
- Young wines come before old.

100 KEEPING A GOOD RECORD

It's a mistake to rely on memory as a record. Instead, note down all or some of the following: the date and occasion; any details found on the label, including name, estate, district, grape variety, and vintage; price; and tasting notes describing the appearance, aroma, and taste. Successful combinations of food and wine are also worth noting.

Index cards can provide useful cross-references

101 MATCHING WINES TO THE OCCASION

The weather, tradition, and etiquette all influence what wine you serve. It is always wise to be sensitive to the context, since some styles of wine are appropriate for certain occasions. In the end, however, the choice of wine is down to you: your budget, your personal preference, the people you are with, and what you are doing. Remember that enjoyment is the very best reason of all to drink wine.

◁ FRUIT PUNCH

Don't use fine wine in wine-based punches

◁ SUMMER FUN
Low-alcohol wines are best in summer, when food is delicate and the senses are heightened. Choose light refreshing whites and rosés, or even some light reds. When large numbers are involved, serve wine cups and fruit punches.

Enjoy modest uncomplicated wines when having a picnic

◁ WINTER CHEER

Big wines are more appropriate in cooler weather. Hot punches like mulled wine and Glühwein are nice, but don't waste fine wine in making these. Don't forget fortified wines: Sherry and Port make warming aperitifs and good dessert wines. Heavy food swamps light flavors, so choose robust wines to match.

△ MULLED WINE

Offer an alternative when hosting large functions to cater to all tastes

Drink a toast to good luck in the wine of your choosing

SPECIAL CELEBRATIONS ▷

Although sparkling wine is usual at occasions such as weddings, you need never be a slave to convention if it's not what you would prefer. Dry Champagne with sweet wedding cake puts many people off sparkling wine; demi-sec is a better choice.

▽ WINES AS A TREAT

Experiment and explore unusual styles and flavors as a way of broadening your enjoyment of wine. Try as many different styles as you can: you may surprise even yourself. Wine makes an excellent gift for casual drinker and avid enthusiast alike.

Decorate box or even bottle with ribbon

◁ DINING OUT

When eating out, consult the wine list, which should give information about place of origin and style of wine – or ask the wine waiter about it. Where consensus is difficult, choose wine by the glass or a half bottle. Don't be afraid to send the wine back if it's off.

WATER TREATMENT

To minimize any unpleasant after-effects, have one large glass of water for every glass of wine that you drink.

Champagne flutes capture bubbles

INDEX

ACKNOWLEDGMENTS

Dorling Kindersley would like to thank Hilary Bird for compiling the index, Robert Campbell and Mark Bracey for DTP assistance. Thanks also to Gilbeys and Mildara Blass (UK) Ltd.

Photography
KEY: t *top*; b *bottom*; c *center*; a *above*; l *left*; r *right*
The publisher would like to thank the following for their kind permission to reproduce the photographs: Cephas Picture Library/Mick Rock 2, 6, 8tl, 9bl, 10tr, 10br, 11cla, 11ca, 11cb, 11cra, 19bl, 19br, 23tr, 23cr, 24cl, 25bl, 26cl, 26tr, 26br, 27br, 28bc, 28c, 28tc, 29c, 29cb, 30bl, 30c, 31tr, 31br, 34cl, 34cr, 35cl, 36br, 38bl, 39tr, 39br, 40bl, 40br, 40tr, 41tr, 43tl, 43cl, 43cr, 44cl, 44bl, 46cl, 46tr, 51cl, 54cr, 57br, 58br, 59br/Roland & Karen Muschenetz 9br, 31tr, 32bl, 36cl/Nigel Blythe 21tr/ Wine Magazine 21bc/Ted Stefanski 31c/ Juan Espi 33c/Andy Christodolo 35br/Rod Stedall 44cr/David Copeman tl; The Champagne Information Bureau 42bl; Christie's Images 59cr; Mary Evans Picture Library 8br; Patrick Eagar 20tr, 33cr, 42br, 60bl; Robert Harding Picture Library 21c; Imagebank/Andrea Pistolesi 37cr; Scope/Michel Guillard front cover cl, cr; Magnum/Bruno Barbey 21tl, 46cr/Ian Berry 58tr; TRIP/B.Turner 30cl; Wines Of Chile 32cr.

All other photographs by Max Alexander, Peter Anderson, Martin Brigdale, Andy Crawford, Philip Dowell, Steve Gorton, John Heseltine, Paul Kenward, Dave King, Neil Lukas, Andrew McKinney, Neil Mersh, Diana Miller, Martin Norris, Ian O'Leary, Gary Ombler, Guy Ryecart, Kim Sayer, Clive Streeter, Harry Taylor, Peter Wilson.

Illustrations & Maps
Arcana Graphics 11, 12t, 20–21, 30; Sandra Fernandez 12b, 13–19.